Our Home in Heaven Crafts and More

Written by Mary Currier

Illustrated by Corbin Hillam

Cover Illustrated by Corbin Hillam

Unless otherwise indicated, the New International Version of the Bible was used in preparing the activities in this book. Scripture taken from the HOLY BIBLE, NEW INTERNATIONAL VERSION. Copyright © 1973, 1978, 1984 International Bible Society. Used by permission of Zondervan Bible Publishers.

Table of Contents

© Shining Star Publications

SS488

To Teachers and Parents

The arts and crafts activities in this book provide the perfect way for children to learn about living a good life on earth so that they can one day live in God's kingdom!

Each craft features a Bible verse relating to God's heavenly home and ways we can work to one day achieve this ultimate reward. Discuss these Bible verses with the children to help them more fully understand how they must live their lives each day doing God's work in order to achieve a home in heaven.

Some of the crafts the children will make include crowns, watches, name plates, keys, badges, banks, and trumpets. While making the many featured crafts, the children will also be practicing such valuable skills as following directions, reading, writing, analyzing, critical thinking, and many more.

As you use each craft, be sure to emphasize the truths it teaches. Most of the crafts can be taken home after they are completed. Encourage the children to share their crafts with their families and explain to them what the craft teaches or reminds us to do.

SS48840

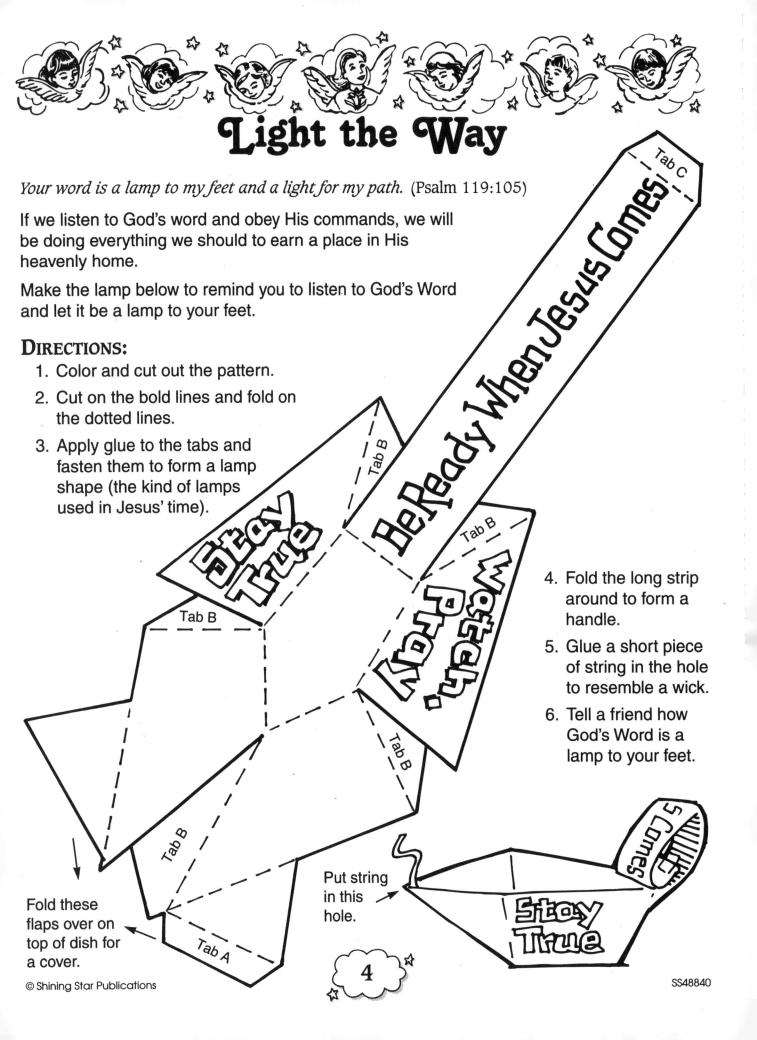

Light the Way

Your word is a lamp to my feet and a light for my path. (Psalm 119:105)

If we listen to God's word and obey His commands, we will be doing everything we should to earn a place in His heavenly home.

Make the lamp below to remind you to listen to God's Word and let it be a lamp to your feet.

DIRECTIONS:

1. Color and cut out the pattern.
2. Cut on the bold lines and fold on the dotted lines.
3. Apply glue to the tabs and fasten them to form a lamp shape (the kind of lamps used in Jesus' time).

4. Fold the long strip around to form a handle.
5. Glue a short piece of string in the hole to resemble a wick.
6. Tell a friend how God's Word is a lamp to your feet.

Tab C

Be Ready When Jesus Comes

Tab B

Stay True

Tab B

Watch Pray

Tab B

Tab B

Tab B

Fold these flaps over on top of dish for a cover.

Put string in this hole.

Tab A

Stay True

4

SS48840

The Eye of a Needle

"Again I tell you, it is easier for a camel to go through the eye of a needle than for a rich man to enter the kingdom of God." (Matthew 19:24)

Jesus says that if we obey the commandments and follow in His footsteps, we will reach heaven. Only the good can live in heaven, and sometimes it is hard to be good. We must do our best to live by God's Word so that we, too, may enter the gates of heaven.

Make the gate to heaven below to help you see that even though it may look impossible to enter heaven, it can be done.

DIRECTIONS:

1. Color and cut out the gate pattern.
2. Color and cut out the disk pattern.
3. Trace around the disk pattern on lightweight cardboard and cut it out.
4. Fold the gate pattern slightly to slip the disk through.

disk pattern

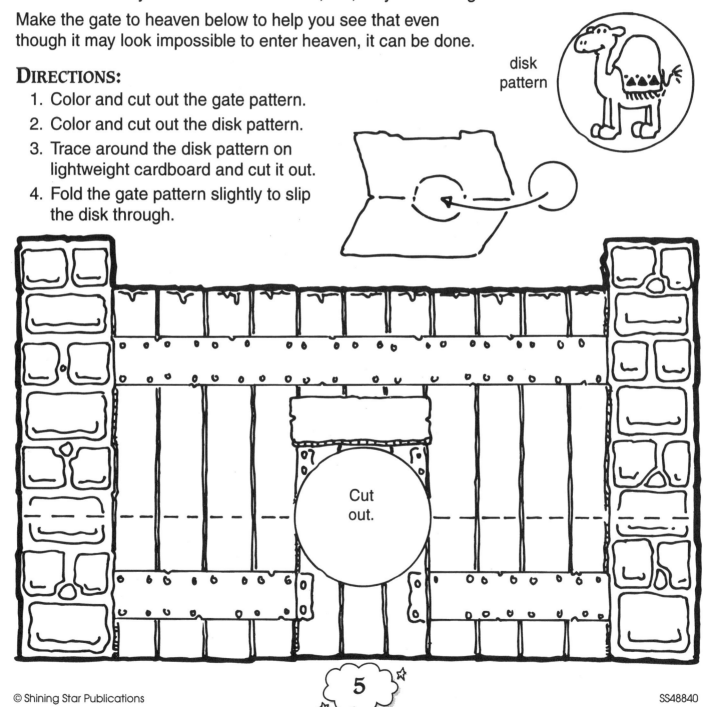

Cut out.

5

Don't Forget Jesus!

I seek you with all my heart; do not let me stray from your commands.
(Psalm 119:10)

This name plate is perfect to remind you to always keep Jesus in your heart and follow in His steps. This will keep you on the path to heaven!

DIRECTIONS:

1. Color the name plate and cut it out.

2. Fold on the dotted lines.

3. Put glue on the tab. Glue to create a name plate to sit on your desk.

4. Don't forget to write your name in the appropriate space!

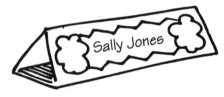

Sally Jones

SS48840

My Guardian Angel

". . . they are like the angels. They are God's children . . ." (Luke 20:36)

God gives each of us a special guardian angel to watch over us and take care of us. Our guardian angel wants us to do right so that we may join God and His angels in heaven one day.

Write a prayer to your own guardian angel in the scroll. Thank your angel for protecting you and guiding you. Then color the scroll and the angel patterns (pages 8–9) and cut them out. Tape the angel together. Roll the top and bottom of the scroll slightly to make it look more realistic. Attach the scroll to the angel's hands.

7

SS48840

Pattern

Cut on the dotted lines.

SS48840

Pattern

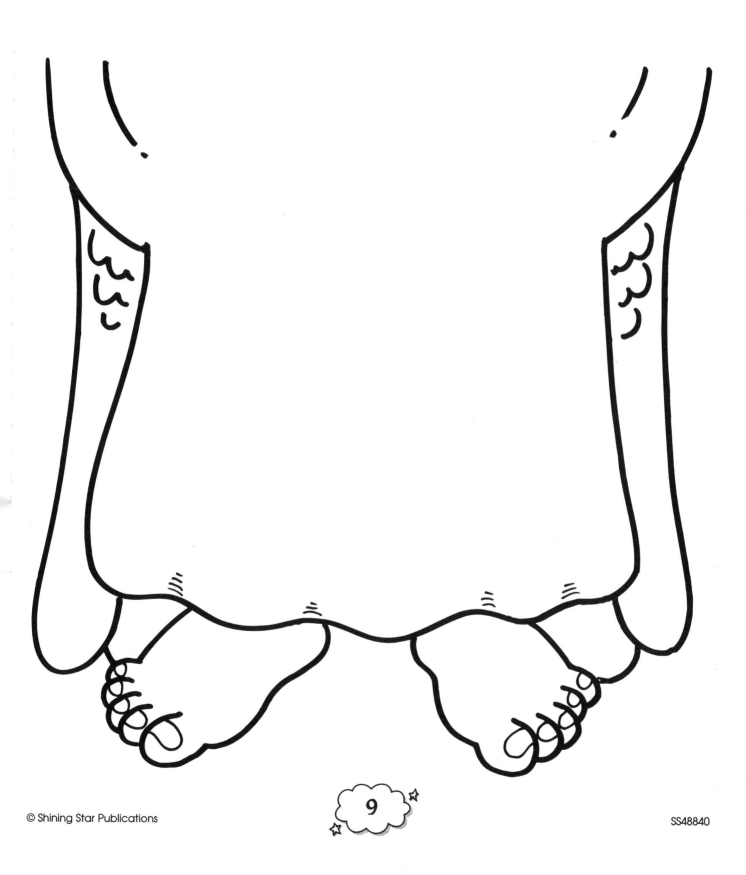

SS48840

Up, Up, and Away!

The Lord has established his throne in heaven, and his kingdom rules over all. (Psalm 103:19)

Make the rocket below and try to shoot it as high as your future heavenly home!

DIRECTIONS:

1. Color the patterns and cut them out on the bold lines.

2. Apply glue evenly around a toilet paper tube.

3. Wrap pattern A around the tube.

4. Glue the wings to the bottom of the tube.

5. Apply glue to the edge of the cone pattern and roll it to form a cone shape. Tape it to the top of the rocket.

cone

wing

tab

wing

wing

tab

I AM GOING HIGHER SOME DAY!

pattern A

10

SS48840

Treasures in Heaven

"For where your treasure is, there your heart will be also." (Matthew 6:21)

Jesus tells us to give to the poor. This will help us gain unlimited treasures in heaven.

Make the bank to use to save money in to help the needy.

DIRECTIONS:

1. Color the pattern.
2. Cut it out on the bold lines.
3. Cut out the slit.
4. Fold on the dotted lines.
5. Apply glue to tabs and fasten to form a box shape.

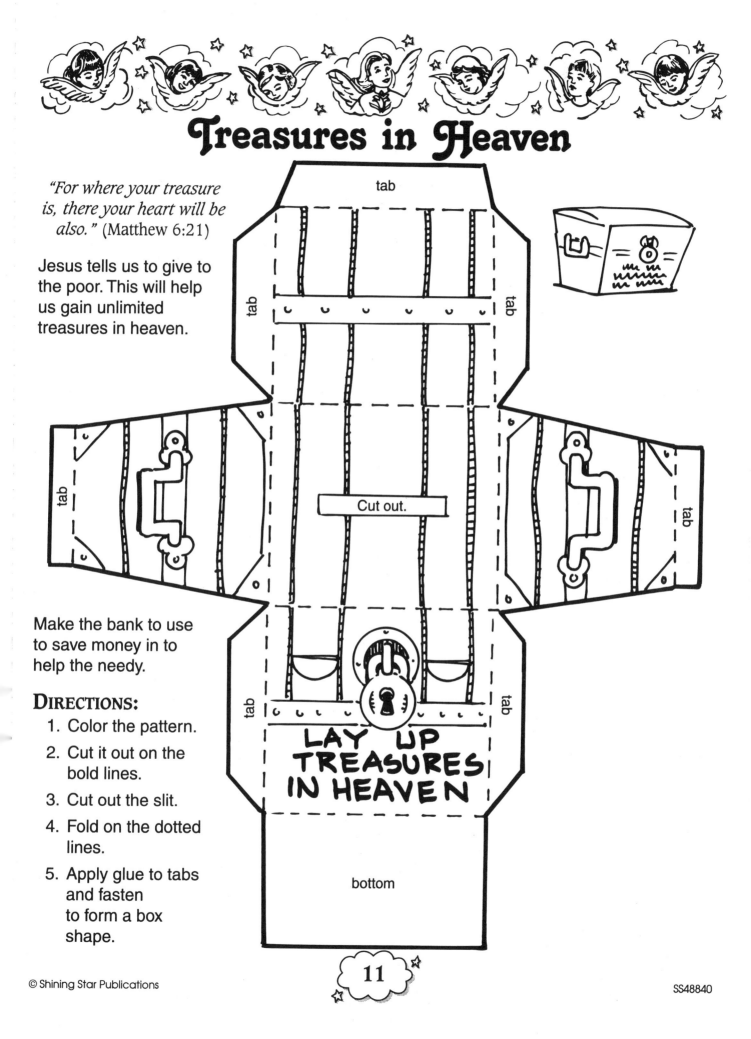

tab

tab

tab

tab

Cut out.

tab

tab

LAY UP TREASURES IN HEAVEN

bottom

11

SS48840

All Kinds of Crowns

". . . I put a . . . crown on your head." (Ezekiel 16:12)

The Bible tells of the crowns we will receive some day in heaven if we obey God's commandments. Some of the crowns include the crown of life (James 1:12), the crown of glory (1 Peter 5:4), and the crown of righteousness (2 Timothy 4:8).

Read about these kinds of crowns. Then make the crown described below to sit on a desk or table to remind you to obey God's commandments. (Note: If you want to wear the crown, the patterns need to be enlarged.)

DIRECTIONS:

1. Color the crown patterns on this page and page 13 and cut them out on the bold lines. Don't forget to cut the strips apart on pattern B.

2. Apply glue to the tabs on each pattern and fasten them to create two ring shapes.

3. Slip ring A inside ring B. Put a little glue on the outside bottom base of ring A and glue the bases together.

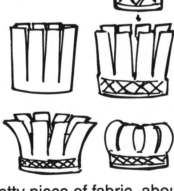

4. Gently fold the strips on the dotted lines.

5. Bring up each strip (as shown) and glue it inside the middle ring.

6. If you want, take a pretty piece of fabric, about 8" x 8", and put a wad of stuffing in the middle. Put this inside the crown to make it look more realistic.

7. Decorate the crown with glitter, beads, sequins, etc.

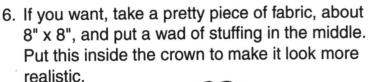

tab

A

12

SS48840

Pattern

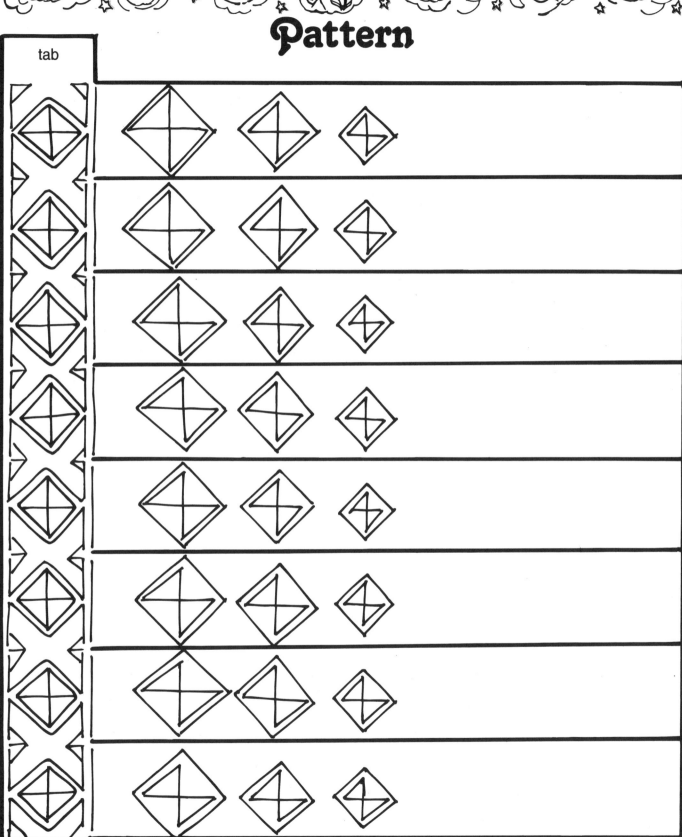

A Throne for a Great King

You are my King and my God . . . (Psalm 44:4)

God made Jesus King of kings and Lord of lords. There is no king greater. Some day, we will live in heaven with our great King. Make the throne below to remind you of the one great King!

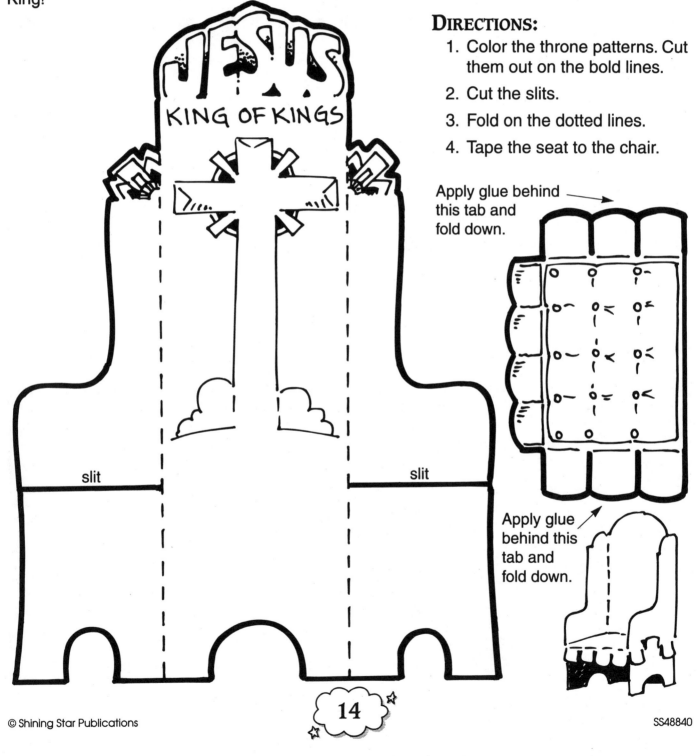

JESUS

KING OF KINGS

slit

slit

DIRECTIONS:

1. Color the throne patterns. Cut them out on the bold lines.
2. Cut the slits.
3. Fold on the dotted lines.
4. Tape the seat to the chair.

Apply glue behind this tab and fold down.

Apply glue behind this tab and fold down.

SS48840

Heavenly Horses

I saw heaven standing open and there before me was a white horse,
whose rider is called Faithful and True . . . (Revelation 19:11)

Did you know that there are horses in heaven? Make your own heavenly horse. Color the horse patterns white. Or color them red (Revelation 6:4), black (Revelation 6:5), or a pale color (Revelation 6:8).

After you decide how to color the horse, cut out the parts and assemble them with brad fasteners or sewing snaps.

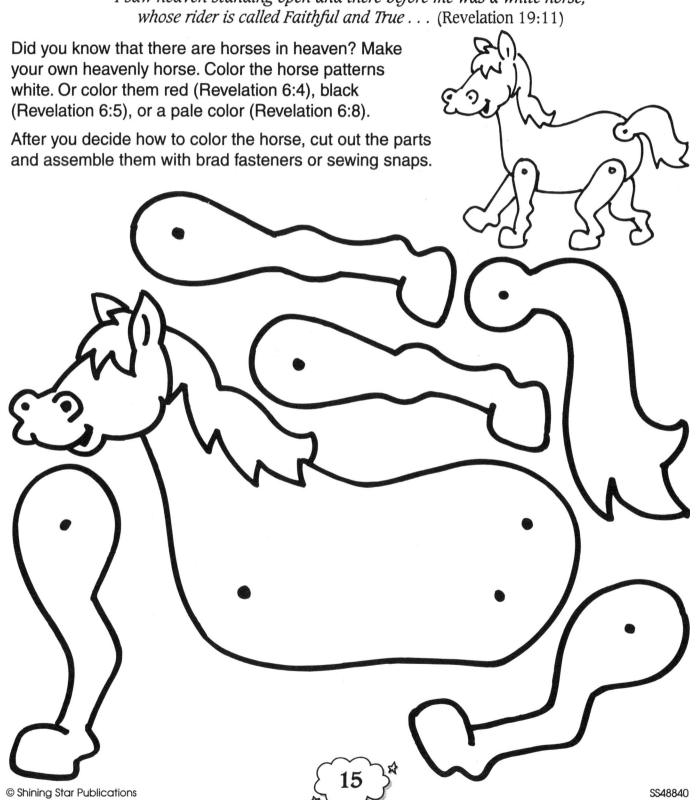

15

SS48840

Personal Bodyguards

The angel of the Lord encamps around those who fear him, and he delivers them. (Psalm 34:7)

God gave each of us a personal bodyguard to watch over us—a guardian angel. God created guardian angels for all of His children (Matthew 18:10). They are beautiful, glorious (Revelation 10:1), powerful (Psalm 103:20), and also humble, holy, and obedient (Psalm 103:21). There are twice as many good angels to protect us as there are bad angels to destroy us.

The angel of the Lord encamps around those who fear him, and he delivers them. (Psalm 34:7)

Cut out.

We must thank God for giving us these special angels to watch over us. Use the directions on page 17 to make an angel to remind you of your special bodyguard.

SS48840

Pattern

DIRECTIONS:

1. Color and cut out the angel pattern pieces on page 16 and below. Draw yourself in the empty circle.
2. Cut out the center circle next to the angel's arms.
3. Insert a brad into the center dots of each circle.
4. Turn the circle to show the pictures.

SS48840

Good News!

". . . This is a day of good news . . ." (2 Kings 7:9)

Jesus wants us to spread the good news about Him. Color the pictures on the envelope. Cut it out. Write a letter to a friend on the back telling him or her all about Jesus.

SS48840

Gifts of Love

". . . 'love your neighbor as yourself.'" (Matthew 19:19)

God wants us to love everyone. By loving others, we can follow in Jesus' footsteps to try to reach heaven.

Create the gift basket described below. Fill it with small treats and give it to someone you love.

DIRECTIONS:

1. Color the pattern and cut it out on the bold lines.

2. Fold on the dotted lines.

3. Apply glue to tab A and fasten it to form a box shape.

4. Apply glue to the bottom tabs and fasten by overlapping.

5. Fill the sack with items such as candies and cookies.

6. Tie the handle together with a ribbon.

19

Our Blessed Hope

Looking for that blessed hope!

A

HEAVEN

GLUE

B

"... Hear from heaven, your dwelling place ..." (1 Kings 8:30)

Going to heaven is the ultimate goal of everyone who loves Jesus. Everything we do each day should glorify Jesus and prepare us for living forever in heaven with Him. Many things on earth are not as important as we sometimes think. Things we do for eternity will last forever.

DIRECTIONS:

1. Color the pattern pieces.
2. Cut them out on the outside lines and cut the slits on pattern A.

3. Apply glue around the edge where shown on pattern B.
4. Lay pattern A on top of pattern B.

5. Use a pencil to roll the corners of the top pieces back as shown.

20

SS48840

Knock on Heaven's Door

". . . knock and the door will be opened to you." (Matthew 7:7)

God does not allow sin in heaven. That is why Jesus died on the cross—to take away our sins. Jesus loves us and wants all of us to go to heaven with Him.

Make the fan below to remind you to be good so that Jesus will let you in heaven when you knock on its door.

DIRECTIONS:

1. Color and cut out the patterns below and on page 22.

2. Glue each pattern firmly onto a piece of lightweight cardboard or construction paper. Cut these out.

3. Insert a brad or sewing snap into the hole on the pattern containing the picture of Jesus. Then insert the fastener into the remaining holes on the other two patterns.

4. To close the fan, push all of the patterns together. To open the fan, pull back each pattern piece.

SS48840

Patterns

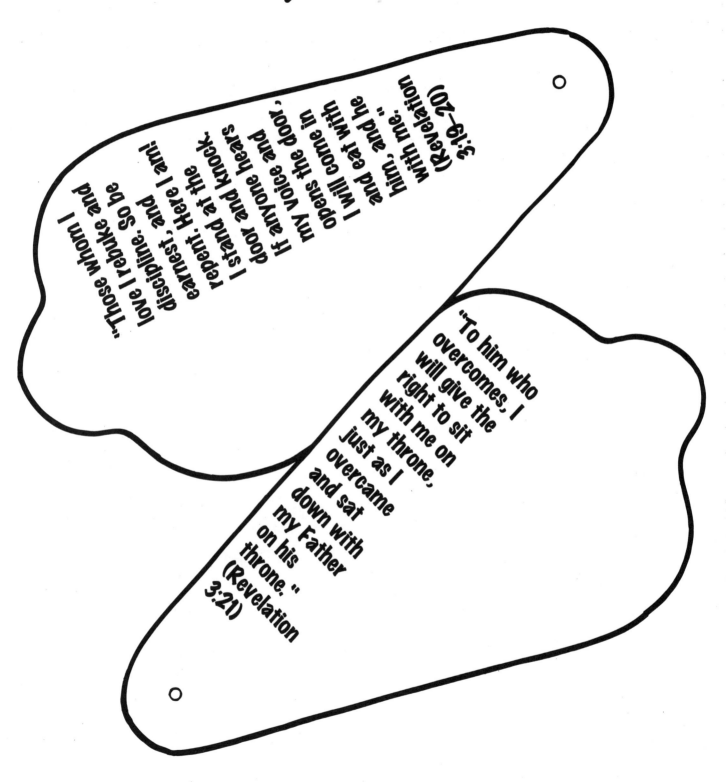

"Those whom I love I rebuke and discipline. So be earnest, and repent. Here I am! I stand at the door and knock. If anyone hears my voice and opens the door, I will come in and eat with him, and he with me." (Revelation 3:19–20)

"To him who overcomes, I will give the right to sit with me on my throne, just as I overcame and sat down with my Father on his throne." (Revelation 3:21)

SS48840

Watch Over and Guide Us

". . . they are like the angels. They are God's children . . ." (Luke 20:36)

God created angels to guide us and watch over us. They can help us do good on earth so that one day, we can live in heaven with them and praise God forever.

Create the frame below to show someone protected by an angel.

DIRECTIONS:

1. Color the picture frame below.
2. Cut out the frame and stand patterns.
3. Cut out the center of the frame.
4. Tape a photo to the back side of the cutout part of the frame.
5. Fold on the dotted lines on each pattern.
6. Glue the stand to the frame as shown.

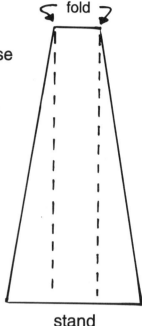

fold

stand

fold

God Sends His Angels To Protect Us.

Cut out.

Glue stand here.

SS48840

A Super Suncatcher

When you walk, they will guide you; when you sleep, they will watch over you . . .
(Proverbs 6:22)

God wants His guardian angels to lead us on the path of goodness. This way, we can live with Him and His angels in heaven one day.

Make the suncatcher below to remind you of the special angel you have by your side each day.

DIRECTIONS:

1. Color the pattern using bright colors and pressing firmly to cover your paper entirely. Cut it out.

2. Pour about one teaspoon of vegetable oil on your pattern. Use a rag or paper towel to thoroughly rub the entire picture until the oil is spread out over the paper. Wipe off the excess oil with a clean rag or paper towel.

3. Punch a hole in the top of the picture, put a piece of ribbon or string through it, and hang it up.

SS48840

Sound the Trumpets!

And in that day a great trumpet will sound . . . (Isaiah 27:13)

Some day, the angels will sound their trumpets and call us to heaven. Will you be with those who are going to heaven? Obey God's commands and you, too, can enter God's kingdom.

Make this trumpet to use to shout praises to God.

DIRECTIONS:

1. Color the trumpet pattern yellow or a golden color.

2. Cut it out on the bold lines.

3. Apply glue to the tab and glue to form a tube shape.

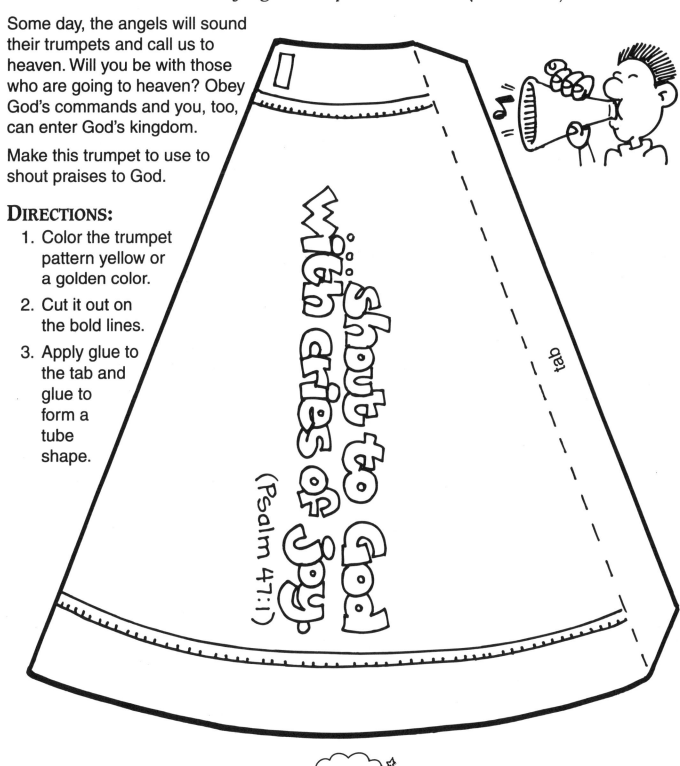

25

SS48840

Welcome Plaque

. . . you will receive a rich welcome into the eternal kingdom
of our Lord and Savior Jesus Christ. (2 Peter 1:11)

The plaque below is perfect to hang in your home to remind
everyone of God's heavenly home.

DIRECTIONS:

1. Color the patterns below.

2. Cut them out on the bold lines. (If desired, glue them onto
   cardboard and cut them out again.)

3. Assemble the patterns as shown and glue them in place.

4. Punch holes in the top, insert a piece of ribbon, and hang.

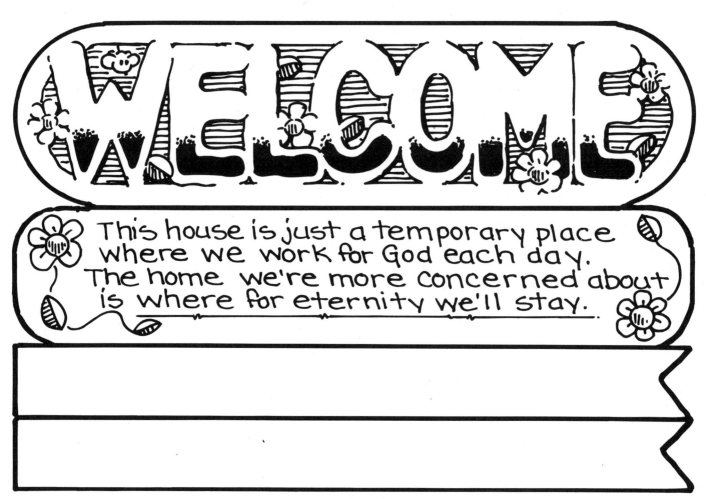

This house is just a temporary place
where we work for God each day.
The home we're more concerned about
is where for eternity we'll stay.

SS48840

God Will Come Down

For the Lord himself will come down from heaven . . . (1 Thessalonians 4:16)

The picture and passage below make a wonderful reminder of how we will meet the Lord one day.

DIRECTIONS:

1. Color the pattern.
2. Cut it out on the bold lines.
3. Fold on the dotted lines.
4. Apply glue to the tabs and fasten to form a frame.

5. Tape or glue a string on the back to hang.

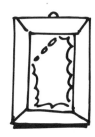

For the Lord himself will come down from heaven, with a loud command, with the voice of the archangel and with the trumpet call of God, and the dead in Christ will rise first. After that, we who are still alive and are left will be caught up with them in the clouds to meet the Lord in the air. And so we will be with the Lord forever.
(1 Thessalonians 4:16–17)

27

SS48840

Be Watching

. . . I watch in hope for the Lord, I wait for God my Savior . . . (Micah 7:7)

The Bible says that Jesus will come back to earth to take us to heaven (1 Thessalonians 4:16–17). But we do not know when He will come back. We need to watch and be ready for whenever He comes. We need to not only watch, but we also need to be working for Jesus. He wants us to keep our lives pure and do good. We need to tell others how to get to heaven. We need to read the Bible often and obey it. We need to talk to God often in prayer. Be ready when Jesus comes!

DIRECTIONS:

1. Color the patterns below and on page 29.

2. Cut them out on the bold lines. Cut out the center where indicated on the smaller pattern.

3. Lay the smaller pattern on top of the larger one.

4. Insert a brad into the center holes and fasten.

5. Turn so that you can look out the window.

SS48840

Pattern

SEEK THE LORD EARNESTLY — JESUS IS COMING SOME DAY — BE READY — WATCH AND PRAY —

SS48840

Prayer Magnet

pray continually (1 Thessalonians 5:17)

The magnet below is perfect to use to remind you to pray to our Heavenly Father.

DIRECTIONS:

1. Cut out the pattern below. Cut off the four shaded corners of the pattern, too.

2. Lay a 2" x 2" corrugated cardboard square on the back side of the pattern and glue it in the middle square (as shown).

3. Wrap the sides of the pattern around the cardboard square like wrapping a gift. Glue in place.

4. Glue magnetic tape to the back of the pattern so that it can adhere to a refrigerator or other magnetic surface.

Note: This is a very simple magnet. For a more complex magnet, add a lace border around the edge. You could also cover the cardboard square with small flowered cloth and glue in place. The angel picture could then be cut out and glued onto the fabric as shown.

SS48840

Fluffy, Puffy Angel

. . . his face was like the face of an angel. (Acts 6:15)

Have you ever heard someone say that another person has "the face of an angel"? This saying comes from the Bible. We need to make sure that not just our faces, but our hearts, are like those of an angel. If we act like angels and obey God's Word, some day we, too, can live with God and His angels.

Make the angel below to remind you to keep your face and heart like those of an angel.

DIRECTIONS:

1. Color the angel patterns and cut them out on the bold lines.
2. Apply glue around the back edges of the angel, on the top and sides only. Do not put glue on the bottom of the skirt. Glue both sides together, back to back.
3. Stuff the angel from the bottom with facial tissue and then glue the bottom edges together.
4. If desired, punch a hole at the top and tie a string through the hole to hang up your angel.

Make your face and your heart like those of an angel.

31

SS48840

My Angel Book

"You are my friends if you do what I command." (John 15:14)

Angels are God's special friends and helpers. You, too, can be one of God's heavenly helpers if you follow His commands.

Make the angel book below to remind you to obey God's laws.

1 _____
_____

This is my favorite Bible verse about angels:

My Angel Book

4 _____
_____
_____
_____
_____

My Poem About Angels

I can be one of God's angels if I
_____
_____
_____
_____
_____
_____

Draw a picture.   2

When I get to heaven and become an angel, I want to
_____
_____
_____
_____
_____

Draw a picture.   3

SS48840

Watch and Pray

"Watch and pray so that you will not fall into temptation . . ." (Matthew 26:41)

The Bible tells us that we need to be careful not to give in to the temptation to do wrong. We need to pray to God to make us strong so that we obey His commands always. This will help us secure a place for ourselves in heaven.

Make the watch below to remind you to watch out for evil and stay on the path to God!

DIRECTIONS:

1. Color the watch and cut it out.

2. Cut through the two slits.

3. Slip the watch on your wrist. Put the end in the slits. If desired, tape it on.

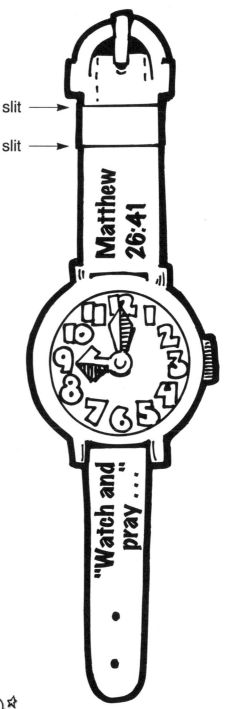

slit →

slit →

Matthew 26:41

"Watch and pray . . ."

SS48840

He Will Return

". . . This same Jesus . . . will come back in the same way you have seen him go into heaven." (Acts 1:11)

Jesus went up to heaven to make a place for us. He promised He would come again. However, we do not know when He will come again. So we need to watch and be sure to walk in His footsteps.

Make the craft below to remind you that although Jesus went up to heaven, He will come back again!

DIRECTIONS:

1. Color the figure of Jesus.
2. Cut out the patterns.
3. Cut through both slits in the cloud.
4. Insert the strip into the cloud as shown.
5. Move the strip up and down to watch Jesus going up and then coming back down.
6. If desired, glue fluffy cotton balls on the clouds.

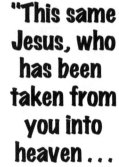

"This same Jesus, who has been taken from you into heaven . . .

will come back in the same way you have seen him go into heaven." (Acts 1:11)

SS48840

A Heavenly Trip

. . . pour out your hearts to him, for God is our refuge. (Psalm 62:8)

Keep communication constant with Jesus so that you are ready when He comes to take you to live in heaven with Him.

Make the suitcase below to remind you of what you need to do to get to heaven.

DIRECTIONS:

Color the pattern and cut it out. Cut through the slit. Fold on the dotted line and slip the tab into the slot to close.

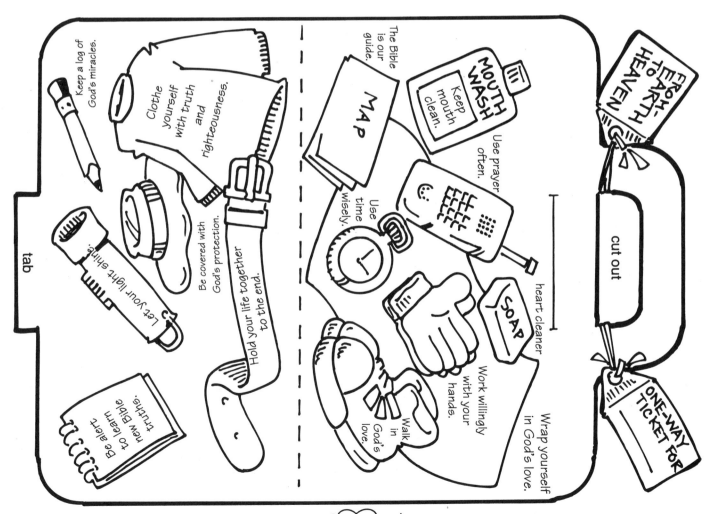

SS48840

The Fruit of My Labors

And we pray this in order that you may live a life worthy of the Lord and may please him in every way: bearing fruit in every good work, growing in the knowledge of God. (Colossians 1:10)

There are many things you can do to show that you want to please Jesus. You can help your parents and anyone else who needs help. Be alert and do your jobs with a kind and good attitude. The Bible says that we bear fruit every time we do good deeds.

Make the book below to remind you to do good deeds.

DIRECTIONS:

1. Color the patterns and cut them out.
2. Trace around one of the patterns on plain pieces of paper to make more pages.
3. Staple all of the pages together at the stem.
4. Write jobs you can do to help your family members on these pages.

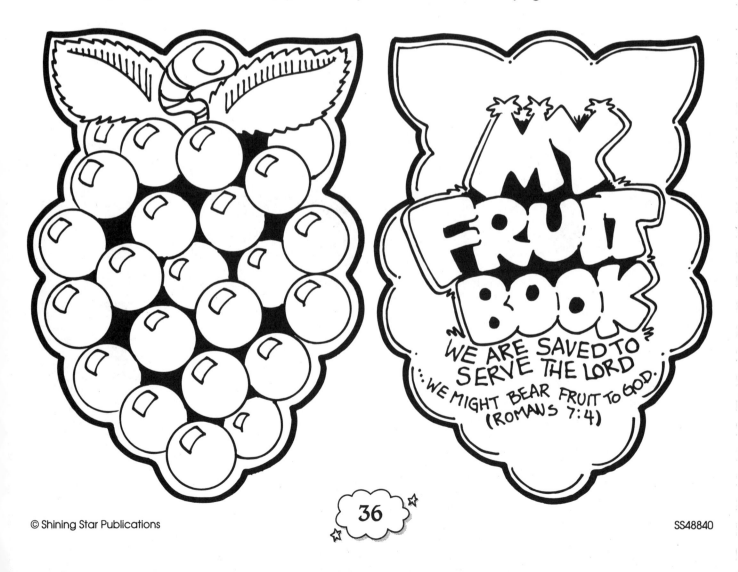

MY FRUIT BOOK
WE ARE SAVED TO SERVE THE LORD
WE MIGHT BEAR FRUIT TO GOD.
(ROMANS 7:4)

SS48840

Angel Mobile

. . . They keep watch over you . . . (Hebrews 13:17)

Make the mobile below to remind you that you are not alone. God sends His angels to watch over and guide us.

DIRECTIONS:

1. Color the patterns and cut them out.

2. Apply glue to the tab and roll to form a ring. Fasten to hold.

3. Punch holes where indicated.

4. Tie string to the two angel patterns and attach them to the mobile. Draw, color, and cut out three more angels. Attach them to the mobile.

5. Tie a longer length of string to each of the top holes and tie together to hang up the mobile.

SS48840

Protect Us, Lord

"My prayer is . . . that you . . . protect them from the evil one." (John 17:15)

While you are doing your school work, you need to always remember that God is watching you. God sends His angels to take care of you.

Make the pencil topper and bookmark below to remind you that God will take care of you.

Pencil Topper

DIRECTIONS:

1. Color the angel and cut it out.
2. Cut through the slits.
3. Slip it on a pencil.

I am protected by angels.

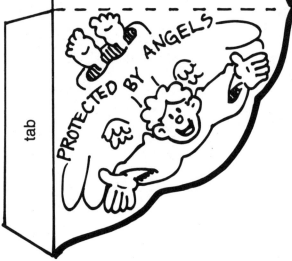

Bookmark

DIRECTIONS:

1. Color the bookmark pattern and cut it out.
2. Fold on the dotted lines.
3. Apply glue to the tab and glue to form a pocket shape.
4. Slip it on the corner of a book.

38

SS48840

Follow the Right Path

. . . let them guide me . . . to the place where you dwell. (Psalm 43:3)

Angels can help guide us to heaven if we continue to obey God's commands.

Make the angel below to sit on a table or near your bed to remind you to let God's angels guide you on the path to heaven.

Fold each page down diagonally as shown.

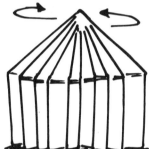

Fan book open and glue covers together.

DIRECTIONS:

1. Color the patterns below and on page 40. Cut them out. (If you want, glue the patterns onto lightweight cardboard and cut them out again.)

3. Use an old *Reader's Digest* and fold as shown. Put a little glue behind the fold on each page to hold in place.

4. Slip the angel's head into the top of the folded magazine as shown on page 40. Then glue on the patterns.

5. If desired, decorate the angel further using scraps of cloth, yarn, etc.

SS48840

Patterns

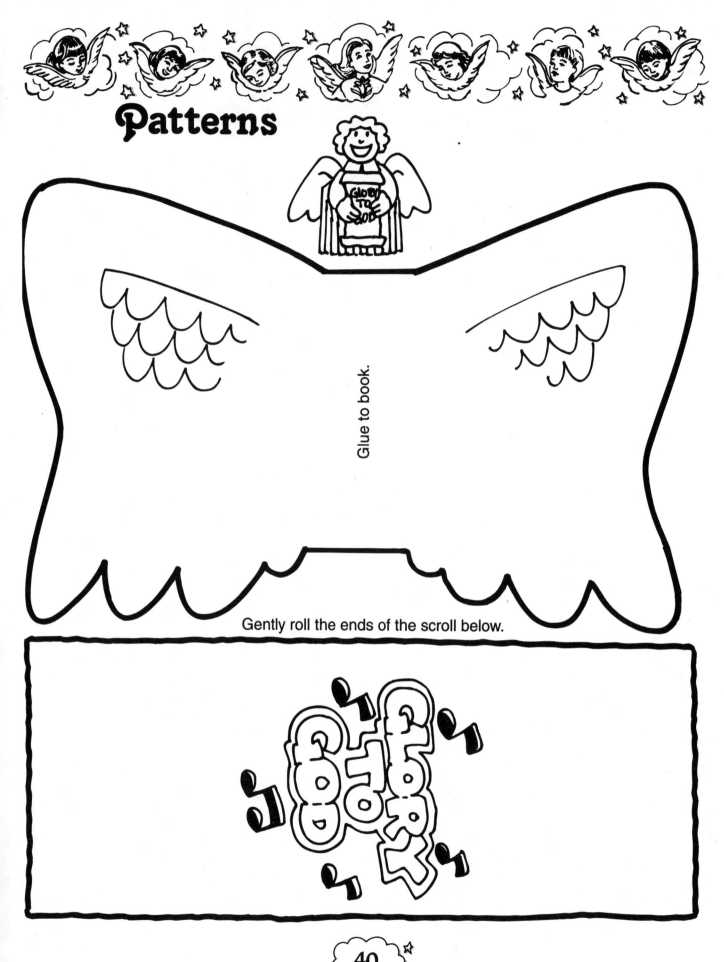

Glue to book.

Gently roll the ends of the scroll below.

SS48840

Key Chain Reminder

"I will give you the keys of the kingdom of heaven . . ." (Matthew 16:19)

If we obey God's Word, He will give us the keys to heaven. Then we can live in peace with Him forever.

Make the key below that you can put on a key chain to remind you to listen to God's commands.

DIRECTIONS:

1. Color the key patterns yellow and cut them out.
2. Glue one of the keys to heavy cardboard and cut it out again.
3. Glue the other key to the other side of the cardboard key.
4. Punch out the hole.
5. With craft glue or sealer, paint both sides of the key several times, allowing it to dry in between coats.
6. Put the key on a key chain to remind you to obey God's Word.

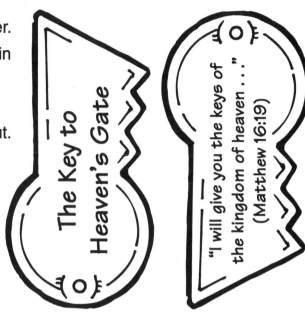

Security Badge

. . . you will protect me from trouble . . . (Psalm 32:7)

God wants to protect us and keep us safe so that we can one day enter His kingdom.

Make the badge below to remind you that God will keep you safe.

DIRECTIONS:

1. Color the pattern and cut it out.
2. Look up Psalm 91:11 in your Bible. Print the verse on the badge.
3. Tape the badge to your bedroom window or door or wear it.

SS48840

Heaven Is Our Goal

The Lord will . . . bring me safely to his heavenly kingdom . . . (2 Timothy 4:18)

If we try our best to live by God's commandments, God will lead us to His heavenly home.

Make the craft below to remind you to "fight the good fight" to reach heaven.

A

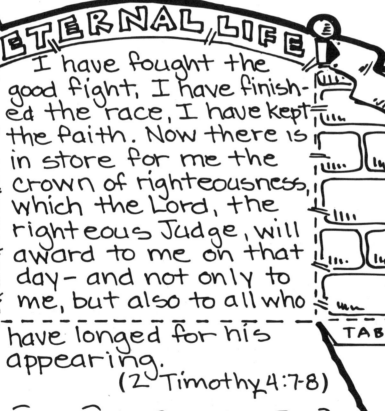

ETERNAL LIFE

I have fought the good fight, I have finished the race, I have kept the faith. Now there is in store for me the crown of righteousness, which the Lord, the righteous Judge, will award to me on that day — and not only to me, but also to all who have longed for his appearing.
(2 Timothy 4:7-8)

TAB   TAB

B

DIRECTIONS:

1. Color the patterns and cut them out.

2. Fold on the dotted lines.

3. Apply glue to the tabs to make pattern B stand up.

4. Set the boy pattern on the road as if he is walking to heaven.

SS48840

The Only Way to Heaven

. . . I will dwell in the house of the Lord forever. (Psalm 23:6)

Listen closely to God's commands! Obey His Word! Secure for yourself a place in heaven!

Make the reminder below so that you always remember what you need to do to get to heaven.

DIRECTIONS:

1. Color the pattern and cut it out.
2. Apply glue to the tab and glue to form a ring.
3. Set it up.

JESUS IS THE ONLY WAY TO HEAVEN

tab

SS48840

Love the Lord

*I consider that our present sufferings are not worth comparing
with the glory that will be revealed in us.* (Romans 8:18)

Sometimes following God's laws is not easy. But even if we
have to suffer sometimes, it's OK because our reward in
heaven will be great.

DIRECTIONS:

1. Color the patterns and cut them out.
2. Fold on the dotted lines.
3. Place the book on the stand as shown.

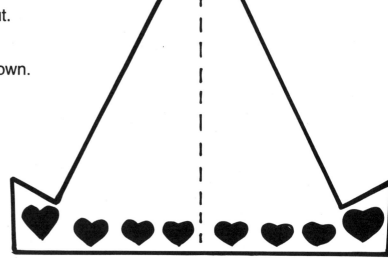

..."No eye has seen, no ear has heard, no mind has conceived what God has prepared for those who love Him." (1 Corinthians 2:9)

God loves us! We love God!

"Whoever has my commands and obeys them, he is the one who loves me. He who loves me will be loved by my Father, and I too will love him and show myself to him." (John 14:21)

SS48840

Praise God

As for man, his days are like grass, he flourishes like a flower of the field. (Psalm 103:15)

We need to spend every day doing good for the Lord. This will help us get to heaven.

Make the pencil holder below to remind you to prepare to meet God.

DIRECTIONS:

1. Color the pattern and cut it out.

2. Glue or tape it to the outside of a clean, 12-ounce, frozen juice concentrate can.

3. Set it up and use it to store pencils.

SS48840

Crown of Life

". . . Be faithful . . . and I will give you the crown of life." (Revelation 2:10)

The Bible says that we will receive a crown of life if we stay true and faithful to Jesus until we die. This is the hope of all who follow Him.

Make the Crown of Life below for the faithful Christian child.

DIRECTIONS:

1. Color the patterns and cut them out.

2. Insert a brad into the dot of the sleeve and then into the dot on the picture. Move the hand up and down to resemble a crown being placed on the faithful Christian's head.

SS48840

Vehicle Reminder

. . . May your whole spirit, soul and body be kept blameless at the coming of our Lord Jesus Christ. (1 Thessalonians 5:23)

Jesus says He is coming back for us. We need to lead godly lives so that we are ready when He comes again.

Make the vehicle reminder below so you never forget to prepare for Christ's coming.

DIRECTIONS:

1. Color the patterns yellow and cut them out.

2. Glue one of the patterns to a piece of cardboard and cut it out again. Then glue the second pattern to the back side of the cardboard.

3. Spread a thin, even layer of glue around the edges of both sides of the pattern and then immediately lay fluffed-out cotton balls on the glue to create clouds.

4. Punch holes in the top of the craft and tie a six-inch piece of string through the holes. Hang it up in your parent's vehicle on the rear-view mirror.

47

SS48840

Dressed for the Lord

. . . *"These in white robes—who are they, and where did they come from?"* (Revelation 7:13)

When we get to heaven, the Bible says we will wear white robes (Revelation 7:14) and will serve Him day and night (Revelation 7:15). Keep your life pure before the Lord. Ask Him daily in prayer to forgive your sins and make you acceptable unto Him.

Make the paper doll below and dress it up for the Lord. Use it to remind you to be faithful to God.

DIRECTIONS:

1. Color the patterns and cut them out.
2. Fold on the dotted lines.
3. Place the clothes on the person.

SS48840